To Steve + Carol.

Enjoy!

Love,
Carol Fitzgerald

Nov. 2000

This Book Belongs To:

Portrait
of a Child

ALSO BY CAROL FITZGERALD:

Embracing Beautiful Moments

Portrait of a Child

Capturing Your Child's Most Precious Sayings

Carol Fitzgerald

The Carobi Five

The Carobi Five Publishing Group
Naples, Florida
1998

Published by
The Carobi Five Publishing Group
3106 Tamiami Trail North, Suite #275
Naples, Florida 34103

Cover design, interior design, and interior art by:
Archer-Ellison Design - 1.800.449.4095

Publisher's Cataloging-in-Publication
(Provided by Quality Books, Inc.)

Fitzgerald, Carol.
  Portrait of a child : capturing your child's most
precious sayings / by Carol Fitzgerald. -- 1st ed.
  p. cm.
  ISBN 0-9641596-2-7

  1. Baby Books. 2. Diaries--Authorship. 3. Children--
Diaries. 4. Parent and child. I. Title

HQ779.5.F58 1998   929'.2
                          QBI98-1367

Printed in the United States of America

Distributed by Baker and Taylor Book Distributors,
Ingram, and the Distributors
Also available through book and gift specialty stores

For All Children Everywhere

Everywhere

Especially:

Patrick
Keri and Ken
Daniel
William
Mary Carol
&
Little Miss Kennedy Kelly

Dear Friends,

This past year has been a special one for me in many ways. One in particular happened at a restaurant with our daughter Keri and her new husband, Ken. As we were seated, she offered an envelope to my husband and me. Inside was a lovely, blank greeting card which she'd personalized. It read:

> *"This certificate entitles you to your first grandchild.*
> *You may redeem it in February.*
> *Love Keri and Ken"*

That was how they announced to us the upcoming birth of their first child. And that was the beginning of the idea for Portrait of a Child. A new baby! I could hardly contain myself. After all, Mary Carol, our youngest of five, was 17. With mine grown, I was now ready for a new baby in the family.

In my excitement days and weeks later, whenever I was out shopping, I'd pick up some little gem for the new baby. One of those gems was a blank journal for them to record their thoughts and feelings about their new baby, observations, goals for their child, and poignant or humorous anecdotes or sayings of their child. Just inside the front cover, this was what I inscribed:

> *Dear Keri and Ken,*
> *This book is especially for you to record all the witty sayings of your precious child. Include the date and age, too. It will be priceless in years to come.*

I gave it no more thought until I read their thank you note to us a few days later. A portion of it read:

> *"We are glad you thought of a book*
> *for the funny things our child will say.*
> *We hadn't even thought of that;*
> *it will come in very handy."*

Portrait of a Child was now beginning to nest in my mind. I had been an avid keeper of my babies' baby books. Why, I kept a record of things most people would consider inconsequential. One of my favorite things to document was funny and warm and wonderful sayings by my children. Keri was ten when Mary Carol was born. As they grew side by side, she kept her own record of Mary Carol's charming comments and responses whenever they were together.

How many times have you laughed at something priceless a child has said? Maybe you related it to a friend or relative. After the incident wanes, it's like last week's sermon, for time has a way of obliterating our exact words at any given moment, that is, unless we capture them.

Children love to hear stories about themselves. Had I not savagely kept these priceless gems, the winds of time would have surely blown them into the farthest corners of my mind.

You may not have time to get the book out on every occasion you hear something significant. But certainly you can write it on any piece of paper to save it. Oftentimes, I was in the middle of dinner or in the car or someplace where my book was not. After the laugh and not one to chance leaving it to memory, I would grab whatever scratch paper I could find and jot exactly what was said, the date, their age and which one of my five said it. Then, at a later time, I would transfer these sayings to their books.

Read what I've captured of my own children's sayings and others within these pages. Let it be just a stimulus to propel you on your way to your own valuable keepsake.

Start now to record your children's magic and tender moments. When you reread them years from now, they will stir your heart......and make you laugh all over again.

Carol Fitzgerald

A Keepsake Book With
Matters Of The Heart And Home

The
Carobi
Five

The beauty of the written word is that it can be held close to the heart and read over and over again.

~ Florence Littauer

Daily Blessing For Our Children

Father, we are nothing without you. We ask you for your gentle and tender mercies. We ask you to protect our children and deliver them from all evil. Please grace them with your presence and bless them with every good thing you would want for them. Let all of their steps be ordered by you. Help them to fulfill your plan for their lives. Put them only in situations you would choose for them and let all those who cross their paths be sent by you. Guard them and protect them. Guide them in all of their endeavors, especially in choosing their vocation, profession, marriage partner, and friends. No matter what their circumstances, fill them with your spirit of peace. Help them to love You, to love themselves and to love others. Keep them safe from the snares of the world and hold them all in the palm of Your gentle hands, now and forever. Amen.

"*God's gifts put man's best dreams to shame.*"

~ *Elizabeth Barrett Browning*

Recall it as often as you wish; a happy memory never wears out.

~ Libbie Fudim

I never leave the clothes dryer on if I am going to be away from my house. One day as I was going out the door, I said to son, William, age 20, "William, I'm leaving the dryer on." His response: "Okay. If I smell smoke, that's the first place I'll look."

You know how most men will drive forever lost before they ask for directions? In a large city once, and not completely familiar with the territory, my husband admitted that he had to stop and ask for directions. William's quick response at age 21 was: "How bad did that hurt?"

T ell me, I forget.....show me, I remember ....Involve me, I understand.

~ Author unknown

Making holiday pies, I had just taken a baked pie crust out of the oven and set it on the counter to cool. In walked William who said, "What happened? Did you forget to put the filling in this?"

~ Age 20

Excerpt of one of Mary Carol's school assignments: "I went to the store to get some papers copied. I was in a hurry and the line was moving very slowly. The lady in front of me went to another line she thought was open. Actually it was closed. There were many people behind me.

"She thought she lost her place, but I let her back in. In another store, I was getting ticked off because the clerks wouldn't help me and they weren't being very polite. To avoid any tension, I just bit my tongue and went on my way. Later, I let it all out to my mom."

~ Mary Carol, Age 17

*G*iven a savings bond for her birthday, Mary Carol said, "I'll put it in my purse. I got a purse."

~ Mary Carol, Age 3

*D*ad - *"Mary Carol, will you hand me the hammer, please?"*
Mary Carol, Age 3 - "Oh! What are you gonna ham?"

Betty Hlavka helps first graders with their reading. These six-year-olds are the light of her life. She relates this story: "Steven was having nose problems, so I suggested getting two tissues. I thought he could use one and wrap it in the other, then put it in his pocket. He said he was not allowed to contaminate his pocket with germs and he must wash his hands immediately or the germs would get out of hand."

*"**W**ill you show my fingers go together with this pencil like Patrick's?"*

~ Mary Carol, Age 3

When eating rice krispies they must have loomed large to this small child, for she said, "These aren't the tiny kind like it usually bees!"

~ Mary Carol, Age 3

*Sitting on the front step one summer day with Daniel, I said,
"Well, Dan, What's new?"*

*"What's new?????" he asked. "I'm in YOUR family." I was
completely amused by his perception of being in the same
family we should all know everything about everyone.*

~ Daniel, Age 6

*When she woke up in the morning she would call to me,
"Mommy! Uppee! Changee! Diapee!"*

~ *Mary Carol, Age 2*

Children thrive on encouragement. *Ben Stein, author, actor, comedian, lawyer and professor, says, "Children who are the apple of their mother's eye, grow up full of confidence and good feelings of well-being."*

The mother's heart is the child's schoolroom.

~ HENRY WARD BEECHER

Friend and young mother, Cary Tronnier, tells this story about her child. "One day I took my four year old, son Joshua, to the pie shop at the mall to get a piece of our favorite coconut-cream-piled-high-with-fluffy-meringue-on-top.

"Just when we were about to take a bite, Josh stopped me and said, 'Wait, Mom, I want to eat the clouds first.'

"It took me a minute to realize what he meant, then it dawned on me that the meringue looked like a big cloud. Oh, how nice it would be to look through the eyes of a child more."

What's In A Name?
How and why do we choose the names we do for our children?

Here is one charming explanation: On a recent trip to the Islands, we met Alvado. He delivered our rental car to us. On our drive to return him to the car rental office, we visited extensively with this fascinating young man. After telling us about points of interest, we began talking about family. A wide smile engulfs his face as he tells us about his precious son, nearly two years old. "His name is Tarik," he says. Then, he adds, "Well, that's what we call him but his real name is Yzahuin Tarik Shamair Hall."

"How is it that he has so many names?" I ask.

"Well," he explains, "His Momma couldn't decide what to name him, so she discussed it with her friends. One wanted to name him Yzahuin, another wanted to name him Tarik, and another wanted to name him Shamair. She didn't know which name to choose so she named him all three."

Two and one half year old Ross was learning his ABC's. Facing his father, he was trying to recite them. His mother stood behind the father helping Ross along by mouthing the ABC's. Ross was exasperated. He finally stopped, looked at his mother and said, "Mom, stop moving your mouth so I can do this."

In Montessori School, Mary Carol, age 2 1/2, learned to put her coat on by herself by laying it on the floor upside down, putting her hands in the sleeves and flipping it over her head. She was quite pleased with herself.

$\mathcal{M}$any young mothers today lament over not being able to stay home with their children, in their need to work. A conversation that took place with my daughter, "Why are we in such a hurry to have children when we have to hand them over to someone else to care for them while we go to work?" Words of wisdom from a young mother of one and another on the way. Sacrificing her pay and career as a teacher, she is opting to stay home when her second baby is born not to miss what she missed with her first.

Is you is, or is you ain't my baby? ♪♫♪

*M*ary Carol referred to her shoes as "shoes-on". She climbed into bed for a nap one day and I forgot to take her shoes off. She stuck her feet up in the air and said, " 'Shoes-on' off".

~ Mary Carol, Age 2

While tucking Keri, age 4, into bed one evening and as I thought she was completely asleep, I whispered in her ear, "I love you; God Bless you!" Her sleepy response was, "I didn't even sneeze." Oh lovely, Keri. You even have me laughing when you sleep.

Kept Moments

First Smile   *First Steps*   *First Words*

First Haircut   *First Car*   *First Job*

When Teresa Bayes noticed her young daughter's eyes watering, she asked, "Jennifer, why are your eyes watering? Jennifer replied, "I guess my eyes are sad."

~ Jennifer Bayes, Age 3

"Every room needs some blue and white, a bit of black, and a child's chair."

~ Sally Griffiths

A story I heard once: *A young child asked his grandmother how old she was. She said she was 70 and living on borrowed time. The child said, "Well, Grandma, please borrow a lot of time."*

*K*eri, age 5, wants a real live baby all her own. She said to me one evening, "Mommy, I wish I had a very, very, very, tiny, tiny, tiny baby." So I took her down the street to see the new month old twins.

*A*t 13, Keri's sense of humor has kept us laughing. Patrick was laboring over writing thank you notes one evening and after several questions as to how to end the note, she and I were getting exasperated. Finally, she said to him, "Just-say-I gotta-go-Bye!"

While washing dishes one evening, Keri said, "I don't like to do the silverware but I have to because it's part of my job, right?"

~ *Keri, Age nearly 6*

In response to something Patrick had said, I planted a kiss on his nose while he and Keri were having breakfast one morning. I walked away to continue what I was doing thinking all the time there would be a remark from Keri and surely enough there was. She was most offended that she didn't get a kiss too and said, "Do you think you only have one child?" Of course, I laughed and immediately kissed her nose and said, "Is this what you mean?" The smile that broke out filled her face and my heart with joy.

~ Age 5

Motherhood: Where children stand sentinel in your heart.

~ Carol Fitzgerald

*G*ently trying to persuade Keri to take a rest with me, I told her I didn't want to rest alone. She wasn't too receptive to the idea. Her clever response was, "How 'bout with God?"

Keri, Age 4

*O*ne Christmas, I took Patrick and Keri to see Marshall Field's decorated windows and the Giant Christmas tree in the Walnut room. Going up in the elevator, a young mother and her Japanese baby, about our Baby Daniel's age, entered. I said to my children, "Oh, he looks just like our baby." After a short silence, Keri said, "Our baby's not brown."

~ Keri, Age 4

Patrick associates letters with common items. Looks at a curved twig and calls it the letter 'J'; takes a bite out of the corner of a cracker - it's the letter 'L'; the A-frame on the swing set - is the letter 'A'. Even while piddling into the aqua bowl cleaner in the commode, he says, "Look, blue and yellow make green."

~ Patrick, Age 3

Daniel woke up one morning covered with spots and said, "I've got mosquito bites all over me." Of course, they were chicken pox.

~ Daniel, Age 8

He was brushing his teeth one day and dropped toothpaste in the sink. With toothbrush in hand, he looked up at me with a wide grin and said, "I always spit out the wad!"

~ Daniel Age 5 1/2

*I*s there yellow in everything? No. Then why do our teeth get yellow? Why does dust fly? When it rains, do birds' nests fall? Where was I before I was born?

~ Questions asked by Patrick, Age 4 1/2

Daniel will often ask questions about God: Where is He? Can He see us? Did He have His tonsils out yet? Did He make Hisself? (Sic) In his bedroom one night, Bill overheard him saying, "Turn the light off. Turn it off. And yet louder, TURN IT OFF!" Bill entered his room. "Who are you talking to?" Daniel answered, "I'm talking to God."

~ Daniel, Age 5

$\mathcal{D}$o airplanes have windshield wipers? How big are jelly fish? Is 2000 hours infinity?"

~ Questions asked by Daniel Age 6

I need two million finity napkins for my nose.

~ Daniel, Age 7

"Your children are not your children. They come through you but not from you, and though they are with you yet they belong not to you. You may give them your love but not your thoughts, for they have their own thoughts. You may house their bodies but not their souls. You may strive to be like them, but seek not to make them like you."

~ Kahlil Gibran

We were driving and I uttered a thought out loud and said, "I think I'll take Busse (the street) home."

Daniel said, "Who's he?"

Of course I laughed.

Then he said, "What's so funny?"

~ Daniel, Age 6

He had no socks on. Bill said, "Put your socks on. I don't want you to catch cold." Willliam pointed to his head, "My cold is up here, not down there."

~ Age nearly 5

William's comment about a lighted candle on the table:
"The fire is dancing with the shadow."

~ Age nearly 5

A conversation with William as he arrived home from kindergarten one day: "I was thinking of not getting married, but now I think I will. There's one girl in my school that I love. Sometimes I look at her and she looks at me.

There are five girls that I love: Megan and Melissa are the first two. The other one is Teresa and the next one's name is Heather. I think I got one more but I forgot who it was. Tomorrow morning I'll tell you if I see her. Oh yeah - it's Erika. At least I know which one I'm gonna marry. It's Megan."

I ask, "Is she pretty?"

"Yes."

"Is she nice to you?"

"She never even talks to me!!!"

~ William, Age 5

Looking at his dirty fingernails one day, I asked, "How do they get so dirty? Do you dig in the dirt?" "No, the wind blows it in!"

~ William, Age 3

Always wanting to be on the move, she will go anywhere with anyone. Will even go to Mass twice on Sundays.

~ Keri, Age 4

I'm allergic to winter. When I walk to school, my nose runs.

~ Daniel, Age 8

I've often cringed whenever I've heard a mother say she had a favorite child. When Rose Nader was asked the question, "Do you have a favorite child?" on the Phil Donahue show many years ago, her answer was 'yes.' I braced for her explanation.

This is what she said:

> "My favorite child is the one who is sick until he is well, the one who is small until he is grown, and the one who is away, until he is home."

A heart-rending, poignant sentiment to which, I dare say, many mothers can relate.

*T*he summer before Mary Carol, our youngest, left for college at age 18, she was having several days of separation anxiety. I would spend hours talking with her, listening to her and consoling her. In between outings and being with friends, when she was at home and alone with her thoughts, melancholy was her constant companion.

As with most normal teenagers, there comes a time in their life when they want to be their own person. They look forward to the day when they will be on their own, away from home and making all of their own decisions. Independent souls! One afternoon as she was preparing to go out with friends, she said, "I never thought the day would come when I wouldn't want to leave home." My heart was touched. I hugged her, we talked some more and then she left.

Later that day, as I related the story to Keri, I told her Mary Carol was homesick and hadn't even left home yet. Keri, who had gone four years through college, who then lived two thousand miles away from home and who, now, was happily married with her own precious family, said, "I still get homesick."

My heart was touched again.

Then she added, "It was a good home, and I hope my children feel about their home as I did about mine."

That day I was blessed by both of my daughters.

"You must speak things that have worth. You must not speak useless words..."

~ JEREMIAH 15:19

There are countless opportunities everyday for praising children. Be on the lookout for these times and give true, genuine, and honest praise to your children. Feed good things into your children's minds. If we tell them negative things about themselves, that is what they will tend to believe. If we praise them every chance we get and tell them what they are doing right that, too, is what they will tend to believe about themselves.

"*I think that will keep me all the night.*" *- after two big bowls of cereal.*

~ William Age 6

A young child, great-grandchild of Mozelle Yocum, had been sitting around one day saying, 'I'm bored,' as children will say. Her answer to him was, "There's no such thing as being bored; there are only boring people." Months later, his part in a family memory album was to recall that memory and then he added, ...'So, I'm never going to be a boring person.' A valuable lesson, indeed.

Our children learn more from us by what we do and how we handle or react to various situations than by what we actually say to them.

"Dear Children, let us not love with words or tongue but with actions and in truth."

~ 1 JOHN 3:18

"Fathers, do not exasperate your children; instead, bring them up in the training and instruction of the Lord."

~ EPHESIANS 6:4

A Family Circus cartoon depicted a mother and her young son out for a walk one evening. The moon shone brightly down upon them. The little boy looked up at the round glow of light and said, "God has His flashlight turned on to show us the way."

"Train a child in the way he should go, and when he is old he will not turn from it."

~ PROVERBS 22:6

*S*pend time alone, if possible, with only one of your children. Give them turns for outings alone with you even if it's only to the grocery store or for an ice cream cone.

"I long to put the experience of fifty years at once into your young lives, to give you at once the key of that treasure chamber every gem of which has cost me tears and struggles and prayers, but you must work for these inward treasures yourselves."

~ HARRIET BEECHER STOWE TO HER TWIN DAUGHTERS, 1861

Apologize to your children when you are wrong.

An entry in one of my writings: William, 18, had just come in from an evening out with friends. Always hungry, he heads straight for the refrigerator. One particular evening he came home and said he wasn't as hungry as usual. He then added, "Ben had a chocolate fit and I got caught in the middle of it." Chocolate stock must have gone up today!

"May the Lord richly bless both you and your children."

~ PSALM 115:14

Many times when I am stuck for an answer, I will ask my children (even when they were very young) for their opinions. More often than not, they usually tell me exactly what I need to know or they've expressed something very worthwhile that hadn't even occurred to me.

No child is ever too young to hear the words, "please" or "thank you". Treat your children with the utmost respect. Chances are they will treat you the same way.

O ur son, Daniel, at age 18, had three of his former friends from another state visit us over spring break one year. Imagine! Four 18-year-olds for nine days. But, the house was alive with the sounds of their laughter. That was joy to my heart.

"I see small children as vulnerable little creatures who need buckets of love and tenderness everyday of their lives."

~ DR. JAMES C. DOBSON

"How will our children know who they are if they don't know where they came from?"

~ MA IN GRAPES OF WRATH

However time or circumstance may come between a mother and her child, their lives are interwoven forever.

~ PAM BROWN

All children have special qualities that are unique to them. Find these qualities and nurture them.

"We are like clay, and You are the potter. Your hands made us all."

~ ISAIAH 64:8

Friend Eileen's Grandson to Grandpa: "I've got the fishing pole; you get the worms."

*T*ake many opportunities to read aloud to your children.
When giving children books as gifts, I've often inscribed the
following quote on the inside book cover:

> "Emeralds and Rubies and Riches untold,
> Caskets of Silver, coffers of Gold.
> Richer than I you can never be.
> I had a Mother who read to me."
>
> ~ Strickland Gillian

*"**I** will instruct you and teach you in the way you should go; I will counsel you and watch over you."*

~ PSALM 32:8

My friend Eileen's son, Chip, at 5 years old was at a birthday party. The children were all playing games and Chip was feeling upset because he wasn't winning. Eileen explained to him that he was there to have a good time and to help celebrate his friend's birthday. Winning a game is not the reason for being there. She went on to explain that she was running for President for one of her clubs. She told him that she hoped she would win but if she didn't, she was not going to cry and get upset about it.

Weeks later, the election over, she approached her son hoping to seize a teachable moment.

"Chip, remember when I told you I was running for President? Well, I just wanted to tell you that I lost."

"What happened?" he asked looking very perplexed. "Didn't you run fast enough?"

Entry in Keri's Journal:

Mary Carol put her legs in the arms of her sweater one day and said, "Hey Keri, do these look like warm-sleevers?" (Referring to leg-warmers, knit tubes worn on our calves.) Remember when these were popular?

~ Mary Carol, Age 3

Entry in Keri's Journal:

The worst word she knows is BABY. So if she gets mad at you, she says, "YOU BABY!"

~ Mary Carol, Age 3

Mary Carol has chicken pox. She calls them popcorn. "Dad, look. I've got more popcorn!"

Age 2 1/2

Entry in Keri's Journal:

Mary Carol said, "Mom, how do you keep a pig from smelling?"

Mom said, "I don't know."

Mary Carol said, "Hold his nose! Ha! Ha! Ha!"

A four year old telling jokes!!

Entry in Keri's Journal:

Isn't it funny how little kids never want to take a bath, but once they are in the tub, they never want to get out. I hate that!

Entry in Keri's Journal:

Today, the mail just came. Mary Carol said, "Mom, is there any mail for me?" Mom said, "No."

Mary Carol said, "Aw, I never get any mail!"

~ Age 4

Entry in Keri's Journal:

My Dad has this thing with health, so he's drinking cod liver oil and mixing honey and vinegar.

Well, he was drinking it tonight and Mary Carol said, "Dad, does that taste good?"

Dad said, "Nope."

Mary Carol: "Mmmm. Does it look good?"

Dad: "Ugh! Nope."

Mary Carol: "Do you like it?"

Dad: "Nope."

Mary Carol has a curious look on her face and says, "Then, why do you drink it?"

~ Age 4

Entry in Keri's Journal:

*K*eri was a sophomore in high school when she wrote many of these entries. It must have made quite an impression on Mary Carol because another entry says: "Mary Carol keeps asking Mom when she is going to be a sophomore. Yesterday, she asked, "Mom, what is a sophomore like?" Or, another one, "Mom, I want to be a sophomore."

~ Age 5

Entry in Keri's Journal:

January 20, 1985 - Right now, I am getting yelled at by Mary Carol. She is saying, "There is no reason for your TV to be on. I'm trying to sleep." She says, "Go downstairs, but first open my door lotser."

~ Age 5

Entry in Keri's Journal:

January 23, 1985 - Last night while Mom was putting Mary Carol to bed, William wanted something to eat. Mom said, "You're on a diet."

Mary Carol said, "Everybody is on a diet. Mom is on a diet. Dad is on a diet. William is on a diet. And Keri is trying to be on one."

She's right! I keep trying but it's not working.

~ Mary Carol, age 5
~ Keri, Age 15

Entry in Keri's Journal:

January 24, 1985 - As you know, we have two dogs named Lucky and Sage. Well, we were sitting at the dinner table having Chicken and Dumplings. When you give Mary Carol a chicken leg, she eats the whole thing. If you don't catch her in time, she's liable to eat the bone, too.

While she was entranced with this chicken leg, Dad said, "She's just like a little puppy." She had our whole dinner on her face.

After a little while, Mary Carol said, "Well, why don't you call me Sage?"

~ Mary Carol, Age 5

Entry in Keri's Journal:

Every kid for some reason wants to cut their hair. Well, Mary Carol's hair is so uneven already, because of gum. Well, she got ahold of some scissors and cut her bangs. She only cut one section, so it looked like this:

It looked pretty funny. But she wouldn't admit to doing it. I said, "Mary Carol! Why did you cut your hair?"

Her reply, "I didn't."

Finally, Dad said, "What scissors did you use? The big ones or the little ones?"

She said, "The little ones."

I said, "So why did you cut your hair?"

She still said, "I didn't."

Dad said, "Where did you put the hair?"

She said, "In the garbage."

I said, "Why did you do it?"

She again said, "I didn't!"

Weird!

~ Mary Carol, Age 4

Entry in Keri's Journal:

I didn't know four-year-olds had fads. Nowadays there are velcro shoe straps. The fad is that Mary Carol and her little playmates in school all cross their velcro shoe straps. It is cute.

Entry in Keri's Journal:

February 28, 1985 - Every time Mary Carol sees the television program, 'Little House on the Prairie', she thinks of it as being 'The Little Girl Running Down the Hill' because that's the beginning of it. Cute!

Entry in Keri's Journal:

Oh, yesterday she was lying on the couch and she asked me, "Ker, when I turn 5, how long will I be?" She was measuring by where her feet were on the couch.

Entry in Keri's Journal:

March 1, 1985 - This morning Mary Carol and I were talking about William. I said, "Yeah, William".... and then I didn't finish because I had forgotten what I was going to say.

Mary Carol: "What?"

Me: "Never Mind."

Mary Carol: Sigh. "Whenever I say 'What' everyone always says never mind." Huff!!

~ Mary Carol, Age 5
~ Keri, Age 15

Entry in Keri's Journal:

May 7, 1985 - This morning Mary Carol went up to Mom and asked her if she knew everything.

Mom said, "No, of course not."

Mary Carol: "Keri does."

Mom: "Where did you hear that?"

Mary Carol: "Keri told me that."

I thought it was so funny. She's so gullible.

~ Mary Carol, Age 5
~ Keri, Age 15

$\mathcal{A}$ sk your grown children for memories of their own. You'll be surprised and hopefully delighted by what they recall that you knew nothing about.

One author says, "We shape our lives not by what we carry with us, but by what we leave behind."

Explaining to Daniel, then 21, that we were doing a memory book for my parents 50th anniversary, I wanted him to think back about memories he could include to be presented to them as a gift. He recalled a time when we were visiting my parents in Rockford, Illinois. He and William were ages 6 and 4. They were running and chasing each other. They came upon the glass storm door. Dan pushed one way to get through. William pushed the other way to hold him in and you guessed it. Dan's hands went right through the glass. I hadn't documented this one, so I didn't remember it. I did, however, enjoy his telling of it. The story goes on.

For many years later he had a scar on his finger, but never knew where it came from. Then, when he was in college his finger started to itch one day. It itched and itched. Suddenly, a small piece of glass emerged from the scar....and flooding back into his memory was how it came to be there in the first place (hand through Nana's door in Rockford). But all the years in between, he never knew.

"Whether you turn to the right or to the left, your ears will hear a voice behind you, saying, 'This is the way; walk in it.'"

~ ISAIAH 30:21

"*Don't let anyone look down on you because you are young, but set an example for the believers in speech, in life, in love, in faith and in purity.*"

~ *1 TIMOTHY 4:12*

"*Since you are my rock and my fortress, for the sake of your name lead and guide me.*"

~ Psalm 31:3

A friend's newlywed, '90's daughter-in-law thought cooking from scratch meant baking from a box mix. The only other alternative: buying a ready-made bakery cake.

"Do not be misled: 'Bad company corrupts good character."

~ *1 CORINTHIANS 15:33*

A s a young woman and before I was married, I taught second grade in Rockford, Illinois, a cold part of the country in winter. I wore a suede coat with a thick, pile lining to keep me warm. One of my little charges went home and told her parents that her teacher's coat had wall-to-wall carpeting in it.

Visiting colleges in North Carolina one spring day, Mary Carol and I side-tripped into Blowing Rock, a charming, quaint town with wonderful shops. We meandered up and down the street and in and out of these shops. One store we strayed into fully captured my attention, though not hers. Every nook and cranny was filled with wonderful goodies. I didn't want to leave; she didn't want to stay. Not her favorite store, at age 17, but, she acquiesced and sauntered back and forth browsing, while waiting for me. Then, much to my surprise and delight, she said, "Well, I guess if you spend enough time in a store like this, you eventually see something you like."

~ Mary Carol, Age 17

A young college-age girl we know excels at everything she does including being voted most valuable basketball player, most valuable volleyball player and salutatorian of her high school class. Not only that, she has inner beauty as well as outer beauty. However, some days she does not see all of these wonderful qualities within her. One day she was feeling particularly doubtful about herself.

Her mother spoke these poignant words to her, "Oh, honey, if I could give you one gift, it would be the gift of 40 years when you will see yourself as you truly are."

Wonderful, wise words, indeed.

$\mathcal{A}$s a young child, Daniel loved to be outdoors. Both summer and winter, he'd rather be out than in. One day, after having been in the snow and cold for some time, rosy cheeked, bundled from head to foot in snowsuit and boots, he traipsed through the door and exclaimed, "My whole THING is cold!"

~ Daniel, Age 4

"And He took the children in his arms, put his hands on them and blessed them."

*"*Children, obey your parents in everything, for this pleases the Lord. Fathers, do not embitter your children, or they will become discouraged."*

~ COLOSSIANS 3:20-21

"He must manage his own children well and see that his children obey him with proper respect."

~ I TIMOTHY 3:4

Children are the anchors that hold a mother to life.

~ SOPHOCLES

Highly spirited, my children's zany antics at times drove me to distraction, but not so far gone that I couldn't see the humor in it all. These antics, then, became the seeds for the birth of Wild and Wooly Willy, a true composite of the four older children as toddlers. Now grown, they are witty and wonderful.

Wild and Wooly Willie

Wild and Wooly Willy,
An adorable two year old child.
Did so many things that were silly,
He could hardly be thought of as mild.

He not only painted the bedspread,
With lipstick and nail polish.
He also cut hair from his head,
And thought it all quite stylish.

With the ease of a gazelle,
He climbed the highest nooks
Ransacked all the shelves,
Tore up all the books.

Climbing wasn't all he did:
In the bathroom he took refuge.
In the toilet many toys were hid,
Down the drain was a deluge.

He turned the hose on and sprayed
Everything in sight.
The neighbors, they all said,
They didn't want a fight.

Onto the kitchen floor,
He dropped a pecan pie.
Mother chased him to the door,
He then began to cry.

On the daily dinner table,
His milk was always toppling.
Wasn't he ever able
To keep himself from wobbling?

His little body, never idle,
From morning until night.
Rightly earned was his title.
He had us all in a fright.

The kitchen floor was being mopped
Mommy said 'don't go near'.
He jumped and ran and skipped and hopped,
Until splash!! Water was everywhere.

For a ride they went in the car.
Chewing gum in the back seat.
Surely they didn't go far,
When it was found all over his feet.

Flowers are a sight to behold,
But not when Willy's around.
Move away from the vase he was told,
But soon they're down with a bound.

On a grocery shopping spree,
In a cart he quietly sat.
Mother thought she was fairly free,
Until she saw liver all over his lap.

He did it with a smile.
When all was said and done,
He uttered a cheerful, "Hi Ya."
Boy! It sure was fun.

Instead of him progressing
Onward and upward to three
It seems he is regressing; Oh
Will we ever be free?

When night time finally comes,
He's tucked away in bed.
A thoughtful tune his mother hums:
"I love you, anyway," she said.

In the midst of playing, active three year old Drake closed his eyes.

His mother, my cousin Lisa, said, "What are you doing?"

He said, "I'm using my imagination."

Shocked, as she hadn't talked to him about this, she asked, "Who told you about imagination?"

"Dad," he responded.

"What do you see?" she asked.

"Nothing," he said. "It's not working."

You may give your children your love but not your thoughts, for they have their own thoughts.
You may house their bodies but not their souls, for their souls dwell in the house of tomorrow, which you cannot visit, not even in your dreams.

~ *KAHLIL GIBRAN*

L et not my fear for my children magnify my doubts and fears until I make them doubting and fearful in their turn.

~ ANGELO PATRI

Every child comes with the message that God is not yet discouraged of man.

~ RABINDRANATH TAGORE

A nother entry: May 31, 1993 - My baby is a teenager today. Thirteen! She looks and acts even older. Tall and thin, she is beautiful. She is exquisite. Even more importantly, she has inner beauty. "Hey Mom," she calls. "Now I can watch PG-13 movies!" We laugh.

Babies are bits of stardust blown from the hand of God. Lucky the woman who knows the pangs of birth, for she has held a star.

~ LARRY BARRETTO

My son-in-law, Ken Johnson, tells this story from his childhood: He knew he was Catholic because he went to the Catholic Church. His father did not attend this church. He also knew there were Catholic schools and public schools. So his eleven year old mind reasoned that if he was Catholic, his father must be public.

*L*ife is a flame that is always burning itself out, but it catches fire again every time a child is born.

~ GEORGE BERNARD SHAW

Teach your children about inner beauty: being thoughtful, kind, caring, and considerate toward others. Teach them to be non-judgmental or critical. Teach them the art of understanding.

"Your beauty should come from within you...the beauty of a gentle and quiet spirit. This beauty will never disappear, and it is worth very much to God."

~ 1 PETER 3:41

*J*une, 1993 entry: Mary Carol doesn't wear dresses! Hasn't worn dresses! Won't wear dresses!

Out of the blue she called last night from the mall. She wants a dress. She likes it. It fits her. She will wear it, says she. I ask her if I can have that in writing. She laughs. We buy it. She looks great in it. Will wear it to Awards Night at school.

~ Mary Carol Age 13

The greatest forces in the world are babies.

~ E. T. SULLIVAN

I am the child. You hold in your hand my destiny. You determine, largely, whether I shall succeed or fail. Give me, I pray you, those things that make for happiness. Train me, I beg you, that I may be a blessing to the world.

~ *MAMIE GENE COLE*

All that I am or hope to be, I owe to my angel mother.

~ ABRAHAM LINCOLN

Matters of the
Heart and Home

HOW TO ORDER

I would like to order the following books:

Quantity	Title		Item Price	Extension
_____	Portrait of a Child	························	$19.95	_____
_____	Embracing Beautiful Moments	·······	$15.95	_____
		Merchandise Total		_____
		Florida residents add 6% sales tax		_____
		Shipping & Handling - $2.50 per book		_____
		Total Order		_____

Quantity discounts and special shipping prices available when purchasing 6 or more books. Wholesale inquiries invited.

Please make check or money order payable to:

The Carobi Five Publishing Group
3106 Tamiami Trail N., Suite 275
Naples, FL 34103
www.thecarobifive.com
cfitz@thecarobifive.com

Shipping address:

Name: _____

Address: _____

City, State, Zip: _____

Would you like the books personalized and autographed? If so, please print your name or the names of the persons to whom they will be autographed:

_____

_____

Please feel free to enclose an extra sheet if you need the space.

The
Carobi
Five

Matters of the
Heart and Home

HOW TO ORDER

I would like to order the following books:

Quantity	Title	Item Price	Extension
_____	Portrait of a Child ·········· $19.95		_____
_____	Embracing Beautiful Moments ······ $15.95		_____
	Merchandise Total		_____
	Florida residents add 6% sales tax		_____
	Shipping & Handling ~ $2.50 per book		_____
	Total Order		_____

Quantity discounts and special shipping prices available when purchasing 6 or more books. Wholesale inquiries invited.

Please make check or money order payable to:

The Carobi Five Publishing Group
3106 Tamiami Trail N., Suite 275
Naples, FL 34103
www.thecarobifive.com
cfitz@thecarobifive.com

Shipping address:

Name: _____

Address: _____

City, State, Zip: _____

Would you like the books personalized and autographed? If so, please print your name or the names of the persons to whom they will be autographed:

_____

_____

Please feel free to enclose an extra sheet if you need the space.